My Request

What happened to me was very rare; it shouldn't have happened but it did. But I have no doubt that, even without the symptoms that led to my diagnosis, my regular cervical screening test would have helped to save my life.

This is my Public Service Announcement to every woman out there to go for their cervical screening test. Don't push the invite to the back of the mail telling yourself you'll be fine – get that five-minute test done and out of the way.

It could save your life too.

Introduction

Ten years ago, I was gripped, like many other people in this country, with the cervical cancer journey of Jade Goody. I followed her story in the papers and online, willing her to make a miraculous recovery as I held my new-born baby close, experiencing the amazement of motherhood for the very first time alongside the realisation and fear that some children have to grow up without their mum by their side. Along with many other people I cried when Jade lost her fight; I cried for her family, her children, and everyone who has been affected by this awful disease. I remember reading her autobiography, written as she went through the darkest moments of her life, and being in absolute awe of the way she bravely dealt with all that this often too cruel world threw at her, right until the very end. The whole nation was affected, cervical cancer was thrown into the limelight and women all over the country booked and attended their cervical screenings at a rate higher than ever before.

But here we are, just 10 years later, and the 'Jade Goody effect' has well and truly worn off. Cervical screening rates are at their lowest in 20 years. Women are sharing posts on social media; encouraging, pleading with other women to make that appointment, even offering free facials and bikini waxing as an incentive! Because these women realise how important an issue this is. Cervical screening identifies pre-cancerous cells and allows them to be dealt with before they turn cancerous. It's not supposed to be fun, it's supposed to save lives, and that's exactly what it does...but only when women attend and attend on time. It is that simple. Yet, according to the NHS statistics, a quarter of UK women either delays or doesn't attend their screening when it's due - a third of women aged between 25 and 30 years. And in more deprived areas of the UK a truly shocking HALF of all women are putting off this potentially lifesaving five-minute procedure.

I live in Bradford, a working class city in the north of England, and at the beginning of this journey I was 30 years old, so the chances of me turning up for my appointment you could say were pretty low! But with a nurse for a mum and three young children to think about I can honestly say I have never taken that risk. They may be a little embarrassing and uncomfortable, but I didn't hesitate in getting it over and done with as soon as that letter arrived.

Women give many reasons for their decision not to attend: the embarrassment, the discomfort, or they may be in recovery from a sexual trauma. I can't begin to imagine the trauma of being abused or how it affects you for the rest of your life, and the smears I've had have never caused me much discomfort. But I do know how it feels to have cervical cancer, twice. To have a huge cancerous tumour trying to take over my body, how it feels to have major surgery, radiotherapy, chemotherapy, to have the majority of the body parts that made me female removed, infertility, hormones controlled by a little patch stuck on my body that I change every few days to stop me going crazy, to have a colostomy bag permanently attached to my stomach because my bowel only works to this point, and to live in fear that one day this disease is going to come back again and take my children's mummy forever. Unlike me, millions of women with cervical cancer have no symptoms at all, and it's at these 5-year screening checkpoints that it can be diagnosed and caught early enough to save not only lives but fertility too. Futures.

So please, stop with the excuses of "I didn't have time", "I haven't had a wax", or even more shocking to me "I would rather not know if something was wrong". If you delay your screening and do end up with problems then, believe me, you're going to have an awful lot more people having a nosy around, and you don't get to request male or female at that stage. I also fully understand that to some women this is a huge deal and I'm not in any way dismissing the experiences these women have been through. All I would ask is that you speak with the professionals, who can help you through the process whilst supporting your individual needs.

If you're still not convinced...this is my story. So far.

Chapter 1

I was thirty years old when my dad was diagnosed with cancer. He was chatting with friends and happened to mention that he could no longer last the night without a toilet trip or two; he put it down to age as he edged closer to sixty, but one lady in the group of friends, a nurse, asked him if he had been for his PSA testing. He hadn't, so he took her advice and headed to the doctors to make an appointment. It was January 2016 when my dad told me he had prostate cancer. He said telling my brother Sam and I was the most difficult thing he had ever had to do, and at that time it was the most difficult thing we had ever had to hear. We all put on a brave face but the next day at work I broke down in tears. I was terrified, nobody in our family had ever had cancer so I suppose I never expected it would happen, I don't think the thought had ever even crossed my mind but all I could think now was that my dad was going to die.

My dad didn't die. The doctors assured him that thankfully the cancer had been found early and surgery to remove his prostate would be the best option. So a few weeks later he went in to hospital for the night, a huge challenge for a man who could barely enter a hospital as a visitor before all this, let alone have surgery and stay overnight. I was so proud of how well he dealt with it all, as he quickly bounced back and showed off his catheter bag to his grandchildren, and the bed mats he'd been sent home with 'just in case' and of course my three little monkeys found it hilarious that grandad might wee in his bed. The surgery had gone ok but there was a problem removing a small part of his prostate that was too close to a nerve to take the risk, so it had been left in the hope that it wasn't cancerous. The consultant seemed to think that it would be cancer free but they would be keeping a close eye on dad with regular tests over the following months. After the initial fear, we soon got used to life as a family 'with cancer'. My dad didn't want a fuss so he barely muttered the 'c' word to many people, including my three children and my mum's parents, and we all just got on with life feeling lucky that things hadn't been worse. I wondered briefly what I would do in his situation, when I was much older of course, who would I want to know and what would I tell them?

At the same time I was seeing a specialist myself about 'women's problems' that I had been experiencing for some time. My husband, Karl, had persuaded me to go and get checked because over the past few years I had been getting pains low down in my stomach. They were mild pains, similar to period pains, that gradually became more and more noticeable and now seemed to be there most mornings and every evening as soon as I sat down to rest. I had also started to bleed randomly throughout the month, sometimes small amounts that were barely noticeable, other times it went on for weeks at a time. Any form of intimacy became unbearable and always ended in me crying in pain and bleeding, so eventually that had to stop too. My periods were becoming heavier and heavier, the pain at times so intense it would feel like I was being stabbed right through my body and I could barely walk. And my skin was even paler than its usual milky white tone, I often felt like I was on the verge of passing out. I was halfway through my final year of teacher training and there were a couple of days where I couldn't even make it to work, but most of the time I pushed through the pain and got on with it, somehow convincing myself that all this was normal. The doctor suggested a contraceptive coil to help with the bleeding, so I booked an appointment to see her again in a few weeks and agreed to have the coil, hoping it would bring me some relief.

That week I was at a restaurant for a friend's birthday but I really didn't feel great all through the meal; hot flushes kept coming over me and a strange feeling like my whole body might explode. I jumped up to rush to the bathroom and as I got into the cubicle I realised I was bleeding heavier than ever before, with huge clots that just kept coming. My clothes were soaked through and I was in shock so I asked my cousin to take me home. Karl told me to go straight to the hospital but the bleeding had slowed down and after all the drama I was exhausted and just wanted to sleep. I was due to see the specialist again in a couple of weeks, so I decided it could wait until then. After that, I started to feel a bit better, the bleeding pretty much stopped and I honestly felt better than I had for a long while. When I went to my appointment I even apologised to the doctor for wasting her time and said that I was probably just making a fuss about nothing. She wasn't convinced though, she thought that it sounded like endometriosis and that judging by my restaurant story it was probably quite severe, so she referred me to the hospital for a more thorough investigation under general anaesthetic.

That Easter we went to a caravan on the East coast and part way through the week it was my mum's birthday so we invited her and my dad to come and spend the night with us. My two girls, Meadow and Phoebe, had been busy making decorations and blowing up balloons to throw grandma a surprise party but when they got there I could tell something wasn't right. As the kids ran off some steam in the soft play area, they told us that the small amount of prostate still in dad's body was cancerous after all. He needn't have had the surgery because now he was going to be having radiotherapy as well. Mum seemed to take it harder this time, but it didn't sound like dad's consultant was too concerned and there was no rush to start treatment, I guess it was just a bit of a pain when we thought his treatment was over, to find out there would be more to come.

In May, mum and dad were on their own holiday when I headed to the hospital for my procedure. I put on my gown and compression socks and waited for my theatre slot and as I was waiting I was approached by a trainee Doctor. She asked if I was OK for her to be present during my procedure, then she asked if I minded her looking at my cervix for part of her trainingasked. I'm all for supporting our amazing doctors and nurses so I told her to go for it, and if she had any other procedures she needed to tick off then she was more than welcome to do those too. She will probably never forget the day she looked at her first cervix, my Itcervix. Less than an hour later I was back on the day ward waiting to be discharged when the consultant came to see me and his first question took me by surprise, "when did you last have a smear?" I couldn't remember but I knew I had never missed one. Then it came to me that it had been at my 12 week check after having Joseph and he was going to be three in a few days' time. I told him it would be due in a couple of months and assured him that I would definitely not miss it. Then he asked me the results of my previous smears, I told him they had all been normal and he seemed surprised. He said that although there had been a very small amount of endometriosis, which he had lasered off, he didn't think it was that causing my problems. "Your cervix looks lumpy", he told me, "there's a rough patch and a lot of bleeding on the surface. We have done a biopsy and will see you in a couple of weeks once we know more". I may have been naive but I really didn't think that much of it. The pains in my shoulders from the laparoscopy were my biggest issue and I spent the first couple of nights sleeping sat up in a chair. Mum and dad were still on holiday so I mentioned it to a couple of close friends and got on with preparing for Joseph's birthday. It wasn't until I received a phone call asking me to go for an appointment the following week that I started to worry slightly.

We arrived for the appointment to a board informing us of a 90 minute delay. Hospital waiting rooms and long periods of waiting around are two of Karl's least favourite things (although he has since spent plenty of time getting used to both) so he went for a wander as I read my magazine in peace. As luck would have it Karl got lost, as usual, so by the time he found me a nurse was just explaining that I would be seeing a different doctor who was helping out to try and get through the backlog of patients and reduce the wait time. No problem.This wasn't a problem, except this new doctor didn't seem to have any idea why I was there. "So you've had a laparoscopy, how was that? Are the incisions healing well?" I thought it was a little strange but answered his questions anyway then asked him about the results of my biopsy. A look of total confusion flashed across his face. He didn't have my notes as he hadn't been able to find them, so he switched on the computer and had a quick read, and then we were asked to bear with him whilst he went to see the consultant. He came back in the room looking nervous and slightly uncomfortable and asked if we had children. I told him we had three and that we were certainly not planning any more. "Well that's good", he said "because I think you might have to have a hysterectomy". He still looked awkward and I just didn't understand "I do have to? Or I might have to? Why?" He shuffled nervously in his chair then read something from the computer screen about squamous cells and microscopic invasion. I'm not sure it made much sense to him, never mind us! Then he told us that the reason he couldn't find my notes was because I had been discussed at an MDT meeting that afternoon. "They found some cells on your biopsy that appear to be beginning to turn cancerous and they have been discussing what to do next". I later found out that what he should have said was "you've got cancer" but I don't think he could bring himself to say it.

The next step was some 'further exploration' of my cervix, lucky me! This involved a LLETZ procedure, where an electrically-charged loop of metal would be used to shave off the outer layers of my cervix and with it, hopefully, all of the offending cells. If this wasn't successful then a full hysterectomy would do the trick. We left the hospital feeling more than a little bit shocked and confused but I did plenty of googling, as always, whilst Karl told me not to, as always, we told our families and between us all we convinced ourselves that I didn't 'have cancer', probably pre-cancerous cells that needed dealing with ASAP and as awful a situation that alone is, it seemed easier to get our heads around than the alternative. I remember going for a meal with friends that week and one of them getting tears in her eyes as I told her my news. "Don't worry, it's not proper cancer, you don't have to start being nice to me" I joked, more for my own benefit I think.

Later that we week we arrived at the colposcopy department for my LLETZ treatment. Karl was shown into a room with a comfy sofa, newspapers and a tea and coffee supply whilst I went off to get changed. I entered the room and the first thing I noticed was the huge leg stirrups attached to what looked like a dentist chair. Then I saw the TV screen at the side, "you don't have to watch it" the nurse said, "but you can do if you want to!" I don't think I'd ever really thought about whether I would want to look at the inside of my own lady bits, so I politely declined, although I later found myself having a little nosy out of interest. Having an anaesthetic into your cervix is one thing that nobody ever warns you about; it hurts like hell and is apparently known to cause women to faint. The anaesthetic was in and I was all numbed up and ready to go when I started to cry. Uncontrollable tears streaming down my face and I wasn't even sure if it was because of the pain of the anaesthetic or the reality of the situation suddenly hitting home, but it was the first time I had cried since getting the news and now I couldn't stop. The nurse who was going to carry out the procedure was reluctant to start but I apologised for my outburst and encouraged her to begin. Then whilst I held the hand of a lovely Irish nurse, who dried my tears and mothered me, and we all entered into a bit of small talk about kids and everyday life, the nurse began the procedure. There was a bit of a panic when I suddenly started bleeding heavily, and then I fainted.

The nurse had told us that the area she was dealing with was bigger than she was expecting and she had done her best to remove what she could, but I could tell by her tone of voice that a hysterectomy was on the cards. So I wasn't surprised when, a couple of days later, I had just dropped the kids at school and my phone rang. I was asked to go for an MRI scan within the next hour and told not to eat anything. I spent the hour worrying about whether the slice of toast I had eaten that morning was going to cause major problems...it didn't. I picked Karl up and we headed off to hospital for my first ever MRI scan. Just the thought of having to lay perfectly still inside a tube for up to an hour made me feel claustrophobic but it really wasn't as traumatic as I had built it up in my mind and I came round to find Karl had made himself useful escorting an old man to the toilet and helping a patient who'd got lost in the maze of hospital corridors. Now we just had to play the waiting game again. It's always a strange feeling being desperate for answers but at the same time hoping for a longer wait, meaning it would be better news.

We didn't have to wait long and were soon back in the same waiting room, this time to meet my oncologist and specialist Macmillan nurse.

You would think this would make it feel more like I had cancer but it didn't. I didn't feel like a 'cancer patient', even though I was seeing a specialist cancer doctor and nurse, I felt exactly the same as I had the day, week, month before, and for some reason this took me by surprise. My MRI had shown a tumour confined to my cervix that the Lletz treatment had failed to remove fully so I was diagnosed with stage 1b1 cervical cancer, meaning the tumour was visible to the naked eye but no more than 4cm in size and had not begun to spread away from my cervix. I asked my consultant what would happen next and he explained I would be going to Leeds for a radical hysterectomy as soon as my cervix had recovered from the laser treatment I'd had two weeks before. Of course I was happy to have the treatment but I asked him if we could wait until after our family holiday in six weeks' time. I can still picture his face as he looked me straight in the eye and said "You have three children who need their mummy. The holiday cottage in Cumbria will be there next year and the year after that but if we don't get on with this quickly, then you may not". The realisation hit me like a tonne of bricks. This was serious stuff.

I busied myself finishing my PGCE and graduated as a qualified teacher, declining the offer of a deferral due to my current situation. I even gained my first distinction for my final module because I was so focussed on my studies in a bid to distract myself from thinking about everything else! Then, nine days before we were due to go on holiday, we headed over to Leeds for my operation. I was told I had to arrive the day before so that I was prepared and ready to go first thing and I really didn't like the idea of this. It was going to be hard enough being away from my family once I'd had it done, never mind the night before too. At this point the children knew a little about what was going on. We had told them that I was having an operation on my tummy because I had a bug in there. Joseph found this hilarious and even now he talks about 'the spider' in mummy's tummy. He's asked me more than once why I swallowed it in the first place, only for the doctors to have to cut me open to get it back out. I used a balloon to demonstrate the womb and how it stretches to grow a baby. Then I showed them that the bug had got in the opening so they were going to remove it all and that the cheeky 'spider' would be removed too. How else do you explain it to three, six and seven year olds? I think they understood in their own ways though and they knew that I didn't need those parts anymore as they had served their purpose of growing three perfect babies. It was so hard leaving them playing at the hospital museum with my mum as Karl and I headed off. I heard Phoebe telling one of the museum staff "our mum's got to go to sleep in a hospital for a few days now and we won't see her". But this was just what I needed to give me strength, suddenly I felt invincible and determined that I would never let this beat me. After all the statistics were good; I was young, fit and healthy and I had the best family in the world to get me through this.

After being moved around a number of beds and playing a few games of rummy with my brother, Sam, who had come to keep me company, I tried to get my head down. The lady in the bed next to me was fed up and wanted somebody to talk to but I wasn't really in the mood for a chat. She told me all about another patient on the ward about the same age as me who only had a few weeks to live. It wasn't ideal news to hear the day before my operation and I felt desperately sad for her and her family but I had to remain focussed on my own battle. The next morning a nurse woke me at 6am to take a strong painkiller that I'd agreed to take as part of a research study into the effects of taking painkillers an hour before surgery. Within 15 minutes my head was spinning, I was being sick and I had to be wheeled down to surgery in a wheelchair, unable to even see straight, never mind walk. The anaesthetist couldn't apologise enough and I think she was probably reconsidering her research method for future patients in her study. The next thing I remember I was back on the ward with oxygen tubes irritating my nostrils, as I tried in vain to remove them, and a catheter which was irritating me in other places. I could just about make out Karl standing next to my bed attempting to calm me down. He said he had been there hours as I slept and I instantly felt guilty for ignoring him, even though I'm sure he will have been enjoying the peace. I also had an oxycodone drip that I could self-administer as and when I needed pain relief and those first few hours I made good use of it! By that evening I had been moved to my own room and Sam and his partner, Amber, came to visit. I watched them play cards and attempted to get involved as much as I could but all I wanted to do was sleep away the pain and discomfort in the hope I would be fixed soon.

The next day I was feeling a bit better and the oxygen and pump had been removed so I was able to eat a little. I spent the morning doing some colouring in a book that my babies had bought me to keep me busy and stop me from missing them too much! One of the male doctors came to check on me and commented on how bored I must be to be colouring, but I really wasn't, throughout my whole cancer journey I found it a therapeutic activity that took my focus away from all that was going on and the kids loved seeing how much I had got done when they came to visit. I even let them have a turn….as long as they promised not to colour outside the lines! It was now 48 hours since I had seen my prince and princesses and I was missing them a ridiculous amount so my mum and dad brought them over to Leeds to visit. At just three year's old, Joseph wasn't too phased, but the girls found it all a bit overwhelming. They had never seen me in hospital before or in so much pain and they didn't like the look of my catheter bag, well until I explained that I hadn't had to get out of bed to go for a wee for the past two days, and then I think Phoebe decided she might quite like one of her own. But then my Macmillan nurse came in to give me some information and she asked my mum to take the kids out of the room. That was the first and last time I let this happen, as when they came back just five minutes later the girls were both in the middle of meltdowns because they had convinced each other the nurse had come with bad news. My heart broke as I held them tight and reassured them that the nurse was telling me something completely boring. I made a promise to myself that from that moment on we were making this journey together as a family: no secrets, no lies, and no questions that couldn't be asked or answered. My children have never had to leave the room while my cancer is spoken about since, they have never heard whispering and wondered what was going on, and they have had all their questions answered as honestly and openly as possible. I don't know if this is the 'right' way to do things, but this is our way.

Chapter 2

A week later, after a painful urine infection, a 'lazy bladder' that did not want to give up the catheter and start working again and a bowel prolapse that was quickly repaired by an extremely good looking doctor and a gloved finger (not one of my fondest memories). We were on our way to the holiday cottage in Cumbria! I had completely ignored the doctors' advice and insisted on packing for everybody, not forgetting the box of injections I had to give myself daily for the next few weeks, and so I slept pretty much the whole three hour journey but I was just so happy to be going to such a beautiful part of the world for this part of my recovery. Mum and dad joined us, along with Sam and Amber and my elderly grandparents. It was a bittersweet holiday filled with the most amazing moments and memories but also a lot of pain and discomfort, frustration that I couldn't do all I wanted to do and days spent in bed as my body was exhausted. We realised that grandma and grandad were deteriorating quicker than we ever could have imagined and that life for all of us was changing significantly in so many ways. Dad was due to start his radiotherapy in a few days, so neither of us was out of the woods yet and although I was putting on a brave face, it was obvious I was struggling with the pain and the fluid that constantly leaked out of me, meaning I didn't feel comfortable to go very far.

Sam and Amber left a couple of days early as they had to get back to work and the following day my mum and dad took grandma and grandad for a drive through the Lake District so Karl and I took the kids for fish and chips on the beach. It was the perfect setting to receive the most important phone call of my life so far; my cancer had all been removed, the hysterectomy had been a complete success and no further treatment was required. I smiled from ear to ear, then laughed and squeezed Karl and our babies tight, and then we got in the car and drove along the most stunning coastline as I cried tears of pure elation. Until that moment I'd really had no idea how much it had all been affecting me deep inside. That evening I walked along the promenade arm in arm with my grandparents and Karl and breathed in the fresh sea air as we looked out across the sea to Scotland. If I could have bottled up that moment right then I would have done but it's a moment I will keep in my heart forever.

Back home I was feeling better and better, dad sailed through his radiotherapy without any fuss, insisting on getting the bus on his own to all his appointments and taking all uncomfortable side effects in his stride. In my head my cancer was gone, I was cured and we could all get on with life again. We held a Macmillan coffee morning that I had encouraged Meadow and Phoebe to plan in the hope of keeping their minds occupied whilst I was still recovering. They did a fantastic job and Meadow even had seventeen inches cut off her long hair to send, along with over £500, to the Little Princess Trust, and thanks to the support of our amazing friends and family a further £1500 was sent to Macmillan from their fundraising efforts. Later, we had the most wonderful family trip to

London for a couple of nights for Meadow's birthday. I was finally pain free and feeling well and life felt pretty good for those short few weeks. But as November came around, I started to get niggling pains in my back again. I searched online, reading hundreds of articles, case studies and personal stories, and suddenly the realisation hit home that this might not be the end of the journey after all.

n a state of complete panic, I told Karl I thought my cancer was back. Karl was as scared as I was but his initial response was to tell me that he wouldn't be able to go through it all again and he shut me out completely. He couldn't cope with the idea that it could be something serious and didn't want me to talk to him about it. I was angry with him, whilst I knew it was only because he cared so much, it felt like he hated me, blamed me, and didn't care. I honestly thought at that moment that if my cancer was back then he would leave me and I would be forced to face it alone. I didn't know who to turn to; grandma was in hospital and grandad wasn't coping well without her so my mum was preoccupied looking after them. I didn't want to tell her anyway as I was scared to upset her again, or to worry her unnecessarily, so I sent one of my best friends, Natalie, a text saying I needed to talk to her. She rang me straight back and I told her how I was feeling and she made me promise I would go get checked out as soon as possible.

The problem with making a call to the hospital is that it suddenly turns the thoughts inside your head into reality, so I put it off for another week until I could ignore it no longer. The back pains were getting worse and I was now leaking fluid almost constantly, with small amounts of bleeding and I was on antibiotics every other week for urine infection after painful urine infection.

I was terrified as I called the Macmillan nurse but she soon put my mind at ease as she told me everybody gets backache and to have a nice warm bath or use a hot water bottle. She reassured me that it hadn't been that long since my surgery and I had probably just been overdoing it causing the excess fluid and bleeding. She said she would let my consultant know but as I was due my six month check-up around eight weeks later, I was just to go to that appointment as planned unless I heard otherwise. So I tried my best to get on with life, and was kept occupied with three of our birthdays in the run up to Christmas! On bad days I googled my symptoms over and over, driving myself frantic with worry; on good days I thought about the statistics and just how slim the chances of recurrence were. It was less than 1%, so the numbers were certainly in my favour. Despite my pain and discomfort, we got through Christmas, making more wonderful memories as a family, and I wondered, could I really be that ill if I was managing to get on with life in some way? On New Year's Eve we had a night in with Nat, her partner Karl and their three boys, entertaining the neighbours with our renditions of the Spice Girls greatest hits well into the early hours, but the next day my back hurt more than ever. My parents came over and my mum could see the pain in my eyes as I tried to get on with my household chores. She made me sit down and I couldn't hold back the tears any longer. That's when she realised that something wasn't right and, if my mum thought that, then I knew it must be true.

I had been sent an appointment for a follow up with the consultant who had performed the initial laparoscopy in early January. I knew it was a mistake because I had an appointment with my oncologist for two weeks after that, but Karl and I decided I should just go to the first appointment and 'act dumb'. So that's what we did. As I sat in the room with a nurse apologising for the mix up and explaining that there really was no need for the appointment, Karl asked her if there was a doctor I could see anyway. He was determined to stay until someone examined me. The nurse said that I could see a consultant but we would have a long wait until he could squeeze me in. We didn't care how long we had to wait; I was finally going to be seen after a long two months of worry. I was soon in the consultation room with yet another gynaecological consultant who said he didn't like the sound of what I told him and immediately asked to have a look. No sooner had I got myself undressed and on the bed, he had inserted the speculum and was asking me to get myself dressed again and come sit with Karl so we could have a chat. "As soon as I touched your cervix it bled and there's a hole in the 'cuff' (the scar that replaces the cervix when it's removed during a hysterectomy). I'm 50/50." He told us bluntly, "Either poorly healing scar tissue has caused a gap, or a tumour has and your cancer is back". And that was that.

weeks I was bombarded with phone calls asking me to go for different appointments; colposcopies, biopsies, MRI scans, it kept us busy if nothing else.. Then I got another phone call; grandma was in hospital with pneumonia and hypothermia and it didn't look good. We spent five precious days at her bedside and rallying around grandad before she passed away peacefully with grandad by her side. Looking back it was a blessing that she had been protected from knowing I was so ill again, because I think it would have broken her just that little bit more. I was mentally, physically and emotionally exhausted when I received a call asking me to go for a PET-CT scan and in all honesty I think my poor mum was on the verge of breakdown. She was trying to grieve for her mum and look after her dad who had also been admitted to hospital for the third time in as many months, whilst all this was going on with me too. I couldn't help but feel guilty for not allowing her the time to grieve. Mum took me for my PET-CT, which is a bit like an MRI scan except you have to be injected with a radioactive substance then keep completely still for an hour before you go through the scanner. You can't even speak in case the radioactive substance races through your body and settles itself in your jaw. The substance (or poison, you could call it) binds itself to cells that are busy and active and there are no more active cells than cancer cells! Mutating, dividing and generally causing havoc as they go on the rampage through your unsuspecting body. After the scan I was so toxic I wasn't allowed near children for at least eight 8 hours, so I couldn't put my babies to bed that night, or give them a kiss goodnight. Instead I went out for some tea with my mum and, even though no one had said it in black and white, we knew my cancer was back. A PET-CT scan is not something that the NHS can afford to carry out for the fun of it. But instead of dwelling on it, we ate, drank and had a good chat and giggle, reminiscing about good times in the past, memories of Grandma and how perfect life had once been. The calm before the storm.

Chapter 3

The day after my PET-CT scan, the Macmillan nurse rang and asked me to go to the oncology clinic the following day. I didn't have an appointment time but they were planning to fit me in as soon as they possibly could. Dad came over to look after the kids and Karl, my mum and I walked up to the hospital which is only a 10-minute walk from where we lived at the time. Sitting in the same waiting room felt different this time. I couldn't relax as I felt sick with nerves, and I was light headed and sweating despite it being a freezing cold day in February. But the longer we sat there, the more we allowed ourselves to relax, and we began to chat and do our best to make each other laugh. It was either that or all sit and hold hands as we cried with fear. A lady close by was moaning about waiting times and how disgusting it was to make people wait so long, whilst I sat thinking how grateful I was that they were even seeing me that day, no matter how long we were going to have to wait. I just wanted answers to all the questions swimming around my head, stopping me from being able to function as a normal human being.

As I heard my name I wanted to run, I don't know how I even made it to the consultation room, with legs like jelly I clung to Karl's arm as he led the way. The look on the consultant's face said it all: my cancer was back. All I wanted to know was if they could remove it with more surgery or if I would need to have radiotherapy like my brave dad to 'mop up' those persistent cells that insisted on sticking around and causing a nuisance. The consultant began by asking me to tell him what had been going on and why I had concerns. I told him about the back pain and the continuously leaking fluid that I thought could be the result of a really weak bladder after all the infections. I explained that I had contacted the nurse in November to discuss my concerns and that she had reassured me that it wasn't anything to be concerned about. He looked her straight in the eye and said "leaking fluid is NEVER a good sign." It felt uncomfortable, awkward almost; there was definitely a bad feeling in the room. "You have another tumour" he told me gently, almost as if he was scared to say it himself, but surely this was something he had done many times before? "I can't understand it" he said, "in over 30 years I have never seen anything like this. Your hysterectomy was clear but now you have a tumour the size of an orange spreading across your pelvis". I went into shock; it felt like I had been transported into a parallel universe. The room was spinning and I couldn't even think straight never mind try to listen and make sense of what he was saying, yet at the same time every single word he said was going in and repeating itself over and over, louder and louder as the room spun faster around me. I could see mum crying as she tried to cuddle me but I didn't want anybody to touch me so I pushed her away and she gave Karl a hug instead. He went on: the tumour was bulging against my bladder threatening to attack, firmly attached to my bowel where it had already begun to invade and more worryingly it had attached itself to my pelvic wall like some sort of alien invasion spreading like wildfire through my body. It was inoperable; joint radiotherapy and chemotherapy were my only option and nothing was guaranteed. I asked him there and then if I was going to die but he could barely even look at me as he whispered, "I'm sorry Sarah, it would be wrong of me to give you the answer you are desperate to hear". This was serious, really serious, and nothing could have prepared any of us for it. I was to be referred to another oncology team in Leeds who would be taking over my care from now on so for now I just had to go home and let the news sink in whilst I waited for the call. I vaguely remember the walk home, I cried my heart out and didn't care who saw or who heard as I screamed over and over "WHY WOULD ANYBODY TAKE A MOTHER FROM HER CHILDREN ?????" I don't know how I feel about God or religion but at that moment I was blaming somebody from up above because I needed to blame someone. Mum held me close as tears rolled down her face and Karl held my hand tightly as he walked in silence.

d walked because it gave us the chance to compose ourselves a little before walking through the door. I briefly said hi to the kids and gave them a cuddle, and then I made my excuses that I really wasn't feeling great as I headed up to bed. Mum and dad left so she could tell him the news and give us some space to come to terms with things and Karl rang his mum to tell her the situation and ask if he could drop the kids off for an hour or so. He didn't want to leave me, even just for five minutes, but looking after three kids suddenly seemed like one of the most difficult tasks in the world, closely followed by talking and breathing. As I lay there under my duvet I wondered if I would ever smile again. I definitely didn't think I would ever sing or laugh again. What would I ever have to laugh, sing or smile about? How could I ever be happy?

I think I think I did all three the next day. It's funny how quickly we just adapt and get on with life, no matter how horrendously it might be treating us. The next thing I had to do was tell everybody. I knew people were waiting to hear how I had got on, I'd even had a few texts asking, friends and family who were worrying as it was late in the evening and they had still heard no news. I didn't feel like speaking to anybody so I decided a text would do for now. Firstly, I had to somehow tell Sam and I knew at this moment what my dad had meant when he said he had found it so difficult to tell Sam and I his own news. I couldn't do it, I couldn't bring myself to speak to my best friend, my only sibling, somebody I cared about more than pretty much anybody in this world and tell him something that was going to rip his heart out. The same way I hadn't been brave enough to tell Dad, I physically could not say the words that I knew would cause them so much pain. I text mum and asked her to ring Sam, like she hadn't already been through enough that day, and a few minutes later I got a text telling me he was taking the next day off work and would be with me first thing. I might even have smiled briefly right then. Then I sent out a text to all my friends and family at the same time, apologising for telling them in this way but explaining that I didn't really know what else to do and asking that they don't feel sorry for me as I was strong and I was sure as hell going to put up a good fight for my babies. I read all the kind words that began to immediately appear on my phone. I felt the love and warmth of all the amazing people around me, a few friends tried to ring but I rejected their calls then sent a text to say I would call them when I was ready and I hoped they would understand. Nat came over and headed straight upstairs to give me a big hug. It didn't feel real as I told her what had happened, but there was no mistaking that we were in the middle of a terrifying nightmare. I didn't think I would sleep that night, but the sheer exhaustion of processing everything that was going on sent me quickly into a deep sleep. I woke through the night to hear Karl crying. I had never seen him cry before and I didn't know what to do or say, so we just lay in silence holding each other tight until we finally drifted back off to sleep together.

Chapter 4

The next day I woke with a feeling of determination coursing through my body. Karl took the girls to school and I began googling natural ways to beat cancer as I waited for Sam to arrive. By the time Karl and Sam sat down with a coffee I had a long list of 'home remedies' - surely anything was worth a try? I couldn't just sit there and do nothing, losing control of my body and mind. I had to take back some of that control and there was no time to lose. The first thing we talked about was diet, I was going to stop eating and drinking all refined sugar, and become vegan. And that's what I did, right there and then, a chocoholic my whole life it was suddenly easy to give up all sweet things and live on a diet of lemon water, vegetable curries and stir-fries. I made myself a list of supplements I was going to buy, including turmeric capsules, garlic, and plenty of vitamins to boost my immune system and fight this spider which was more of a tarantula this time around.

Then we took Joseph to a play place and the men took it in turns to dive into the ball pits and down the slides with him as I continued with my research. The conversation turned to cannabis oil, could we? Should we? Does it even work? Karl asked around and a friend of a friend knew somebody who could get us some to try that was apparently pure and top quality. But it was over £100 a time and for it to have any chance of success I would need around 10. Sam said if we got some then he would make sure we could afford the rest. It arrived that night, thick black tar like stuff in a plastic syringe; it was seriously sticky and smelt so strong my head felt dizzy just from having a quick sniff! I had done my research on how it should be used, building up gradually starting with the tiniest little dot rubbed on my gums or under my tongue. I have barely even touched a cigarette in my life, never mind anything stronger so I wasn't sure how I was going to react but I couldn't see how the tiniest little pin prick sized amount could cause too much of an issue? It tasted weird, kind of like 'weed' smells I guess, even the tiniest bit left the strongest taste in my mouth and Karl laughed at the smell of my breath! I tried, for a couple of weeks I really tried, but I just couldn't deal with how it made me feel. I felt dizzy, paranoid and sick and as though my whole body was going left which amused Karl greatly as I shouted "I'm going left again!" So I decided it was best for now to stick to the diet and supplements and in the end we gave the oil to a friend who had a family member who was suffering unbearable pain as a result of terminal cancer. I just hope it helped her find some peace and comfort towards the end.

My first visit to Leeds to meet with my new oncologist came around quickly. Mum and Karl came again and this time we were all just eager to find out what the plan of action was and when treatment would begin. This time I had a female oncologist and she seemed really nice and straight to the point. She told us that the worry was that this was an aggressive and rare type of cancer because of how fast it was growing and spreading, although my previous biopsies had never appeared to suggest this. She also told us that she'd had her own team look at my MRI scans and they weren't convinced that the tumour had in fact attached to my pelvic wall – it was definitely touching but maybe not attached - and this tiny bit of information suddenly made a huge amount of difference. Although we knew the tumour was already firmly attached and invading my bowel, if it wasn't yet invading my bladder and pelvic wall then I had more hope and more chance of survival. But there were still lots of 'ifs' and 'buts' and things that didn't add up. "I want to do my own investigations" the oncologist told us, "I want to look at every scan from the very first cancer diagnosis. I want my team to retest every biopsy you've had, even your complete hysterectomy". I had visions of my womb being hauled out of a freezer and popped in the microwave to defrost like a joint of meat. "I've requested every bit of information from Bradford and I want to put you to sleep to take my own biopsies and find out just what we are dealing with". Then she asked "By the way, have you ever smoked?" She seemed very pleased when I said no. It was a lot later into my treatment that she told me my chances of survival were greatly increased by the fact I have never smoked. Cervical cancer cells are very similar to lung cancer cells and easily damaged by the chemicals in cigarettes, resulting in them not responding to chemotherapy or radiotherapy very well in smokers. At that point I still didn't know what my treatment would be or when it would begin, but at least we were moving in the right direction.

My oldest and closest friend, Gina, arrived from Australia to see me. Seriously, what sort of an amazing friend drops everything, takes time off work and flies around the world to be by your side? We were all so excited to see her, despite the circumstances, and a few days later she was with us as we laid my beautiful Grandma to rest. I had written the eulogy with mum but with thoughts of my cancerous body filling my head I was worried that I just wouldn't be able to stand up and say the words out loud. So I decided to take a couple of anxiety pills that my sister-in-law had given me to calm me down. They seemed to work as I stood next to my beautiful strong mummy and spoke. We both cried a little but these were tears for Grandma - this was her day and a beautiful day shared with friends and family. The next day was a bad day though. Gina came round in the day and I wasn't feeling myself, I was in so much pain, especially in my stomach, and I felt like giving up. I lay on the sofa with a hot water bottle feeling completely useless and sorry for myself. Later in the evening, Karl was upstairs putting the kids to bed and I started to panic. The pain throughout my body was becoming more and more intense, I felt like I was on fire, and I thought I was dying there and then. I shouted for Karl and then I rang my mum, who was trying to calm me down over the phone, but it wasn't working so she told me she would be right over. Karl had never seen me like this; I had never been like this. I screamed that I couldn't breathe, the pain becoming more unbearable, as he phoned an ambulance because he didn't know what else to do. That was my first ever real panic attack and I wouldn't wish it on anybody, the paramedics and my parents arrived and everybody tried to calm me down. They all said it was a normal reaction to all I was going through but nothing about it felt normal to me. I eventually calmed down and apologised to the paramedics for wasting their time, but they told me not to worry and that

I could call them or go to the hospital any time I wanted and that I wouldn't be wasting anybody's time.

A few days later, in agony with stomach cramps again, my mum took me to A&E. As I lay on the bed, the pain got more and more intense and I was beside myself, rolling around the bed, up and down, trying to make the pain go away. Years ago, when I broke my arm, I had a reaction to morphine so I had always avoided it saying I was allergic. But at some point during my hysterectomy recovery, I had been given some liquid morphine and I had been absolutely fine, so this time when they offered me morphine intravenously I didn't object. Soon, huge white lumps were appearing all over my body, itching so intensely I could have ripped my skin right off. It turns out I do react to morphine, intravenously anyway. The nurse quickly pushed water through my veins to flush out the effects of the morphine and the itching calmed but the agony in my stomach remained the same. Nobody knew what to do; I think they presumed, as we did, that the pain was related to the cancer. I was in Leeds the next day for my complete examination under anaesthetic, so the plan was just to keep me as calm as possible overnight then ship me straight over to Leeds the next day. My mum was struggling to hold back the tears as I begged and begged for somebody to just take the pain away. I cried that I didn't want to have to deal with any of it any more. Then a doctor asked if anybody had tried giving me a muscle relaxant, seeing as none of the pain relief I had been given had touched the surface. She gave me some Buscopan and within minutes the pain finally started to ease. I don't know why my bowel had gone into spasm like it had, it could well have been down to the tumour or maybe my anxiety, change in diet or medication, but I was just so relieved it had stopped. That night, the hospital was full to bursting but they wanted to keep a close eye on me, so I was given a bed on a ward for elderly males, albeit with my own room.

I was still exhausted when I arrived at Leeds the next day so I was quite happy to be sent straight down for my drug-induced nap. When I came round, mum and I were shown in to a small room where we were to wait for further information. Two older women patients were in there too, one waiting for a procedure; one recovering like me. One of the ladies began to tell the other that she had finished her treatment but her tumour hadn't shrunk one bit, so she wasn't sure what was next for her. She was so matter of fact as she said another lady who had started treatment at the same time as her was doing really well and her tumour had shrunk a lot, but she hadn't responded to treatment at all. Of course I felt very sad for this lady but my anxiety was beginning to take over again and I asked my mum to get me out of there. I couldn't deal with it at that moment and the last thing I wanted was another panic attack.

We were waiting in the main waiting room when the consultant called us in to a tiny little room, I don't think you could even call it an office, more of a cupboard, and she sat on a small coffee table as she spoke to us. She had taken further biopsies which had been sent for urgent testing and in her words she had "got right in and given the tumour a good wiggle". "It wiggles!" she announced, like I had presented her with my first wobbly tooth, but the excitement in her voice told me this must be a good thing. "The tumour is not attached to your pelvic wall, Sarah, I can hold it and move it freely. It is only attached to your bowel." Of course this was good news but it didn't change my treatment plan or the fact that there was a long way to go and a very real chance I might not survive this, but I guess it gave us all a little bit of hope. She said she would be in touch in a day or two once she had the biopsy results and then we would finally get a date for treatment to start. So off we went home again for more waiting, and more vegetable curry and lemon water.

She rang the next day to tell me that all my results looked 'good', the cancer was just your average, most common type and apparently my hysterectomy really was completely clear with not a single cell of cancer anywhere to be seen. I struggled to get my head round this; I still do now if I'm honest although I've lost count of the number of times we have talked about it with different oncology staff. I understand that what happened to me was extremely rare and unusual and shouldn't have happened, and I understand that nobody really knows exactly how or why as it's very complex and the human body is a funny old thing sometimes. But none of this satisfies my need to get my head around the fact that, just five short months after having a completely clear hysterectomy and MRI and being declared cancer free, I could now have a cancerous tumour the size of an orange invading my body. Where did it appear from? How did it grow so quickly? Even now, nobody really knows, and at the time they had no idea how quickly it would continue to spread or whether it would respond at all to chemotherapy or radiotherapy, in reality it just shouldn't have been there so how could anybody know what it was likely to do next. But more good news was that my tumour hadn't grown at all over the past month of investigations, which was another fact to baffle our brains a little more. Why had it suddenly stopped growing? I had only had the smallest amount of cannabis oil - although, of course I didn't tell the doctors about that - so that couldn't be it. "It must be my new diet!" I declared, "I'm not eating enough sugar to feed it". It gave us an explanation for something at least, whether it was the right one or not.

I was eager to know when my treatment would start and how long it would last. We had been told it would be in February so that meant the next week or two at the latest. But again, things were not quite straightforward, as tends to be the case with me. The consultant told me she had been having a think about my bowel issues and she was really concerned that if the tumour began to shrink, it would rip a hole in my bowel. If this was to happen I would be in serious trouble. This alone could kill me and at the very least it would mean my treatment would have to be stopped halfway through the course, jeopardising the effect it was having, whilst I had emergency surgery to deal with my bowel. So she had spoken to a consultant in Bradford and I would be having an operation to have my bowel redirected, out of my stomach, with a bag attached. It might be temporary, it could be permanent, just something else nobody really knew the answer to, but I had to have it done and soon. How do you even begin to process so much information all at once? I just said OK and that I would pack a hospital bag and wait again for the call.

Chapter 5

We didn't have any time to get used to the news I would be having a colostomy as the following day I received a phone call asking for me to go for a pre-op, as my operation would be in three days' time. With everything else that was going on, this all seemed like nothing, routine almost, just something to get done and out of the way so we could get on with the important stuff; starting treatment and fighting back. I don't remember even thinking about what it would be like living with a bag or how long I might have it for: I had to have it and that was that. There was no other option as the alternative was to risk the life I planned to fight so hard to keep. I was having this operation at Bradford Royal Infirmary as I would be in hospital for around ten days so I needed to be near to my family. I don't remember arriving at the hospital or going for the operation, by this point I was on autopilot, making sure the kids were sorted (Karl is perfectly capable of doing this but I am an absolute self-confessed control freak when it comes to the house and kids!), telling friends and family where they could find me for the next week or so and wondering, all day, every day, when would treatment start? Would it work? Would the tumour do any more damage in the mean time? I can guarantee though that on waking from this operation, like every other I have ever had, I will have caused chaos in the recovery room, shouting, crying and fighting my way off the bed like a crazed animal in the zoo. The theatre staff are always grateful that I warn them before-hand so they know just what to expect, as they pin me down to the bed for my own safety until the effect of the anaesthetic wears off.

Then I was taken to a side room where a lovely elderly lady was in the next bed and once I was awake enough and the painkillers were working their magic, we had a good chat. It felt nice to talk to somebody who had no idea about all that I was going through; she didn't ask and I didn't tell. We just chatted about everyday things, such as life, families, work, like 'normal' people. But the next day I wished her well as she was replaced by another lady. I had a few visitors and of course Karl and my babies came after school every day and kept me entertained for an hour or so, telling me tales about what they had been up to and the silly things daddy had been doing to make them laugh. Karl's work was very understanding and let him work his hours around the kids so that he could do school drop offs and pickups with both of our parents helping out too. Every morning and night I would get phone calls, pictures and videos to put a smile on my face, especially on World Book Day when Karl did an amazing job of transforming them into characters from their favourite stories. I was so proud of how well they were all getting on with things and, despite the circumstances, Karl was really enjoying some quality daddy time with the kids, without mummy interfering and taking over as always! I remember on one visit we were all sitting downstairs on benches and the kids all went and sat with their daddy, fighting to get on his knee, whilst I sat opposite on my own. This comforted me knowing that if the worst were to happen, my family would all stick together and get each other through it. As heart-breaking it would be for them all; they could and would survive without me.

I was doing OK with my new 'bag'. I had to have another catheter briefly, which filled me with dread, but it wasn't too bad and wasn't in for long. I spent my days reading and colouring and every other day I would have a visit from my new stoma nurse to help me clean my stitches and change my bag and she always seemed pleased with my progress. On the third day I got another new 'roomie', who, in her own words "had got stomach pain after eating fish and chips". She asked me on more than one occasion why I thought it had happened and if I had ever experienced it myself. She kept me entertained to say the least, although 'infuriated' would be a better word! Talking on the phone at all hours, pressing the call button constantly for the most ridiculous reasons and demands and one morning she woke me up at 4am to ask if she could borrow my head phones as she couldn't sleep. Then on Friday, when she was due to have her scan, she accidentally ate a sandwich so it was announced she would be with me for the weekend, lucky me! On Saturday afternoon I had lots of visitors, a friend had come up from London to stay with family and visit me and another had driven three hours just to come sit at my bedside. I felt like the luckiest girl in the world with all this love and support surrounding me. So many of my friends came that there was no room at my bedside, so we went down to the hospital café where we talked and laughed for a good couple of hours until I could barely keep my eyes open so we reluctantly said our goodbyes.

My friend Emma walked me back to the ward and we arrived to an announcement that I was moving beds! I didn't ask why, just got Emma to help me pack my things up quickly before they changed their minds. I said goodbye to my 'friend' and added a little prayer in my head for the next poor patient who would be left to deal with her, then we followed the nurse to my new bed, right at the end of a long ward. There were certainly some characters in this ward. A few of the women knew each other well and it seemed they had been here a significant length of time. One girl about my age would go home to be with her family through the day but had to come back every night for treatment -I don't know how long this was for but it made me really sad. It was like being in a room of naughty school girls, with talk of orgies and men coming in through the night. Not what you expect from ladies in their seventies and eighties stuck in hospital, but it really made me smile as I read my book and relaxed the best I could. I drifted off for an hour or so before waking up just before midnight to a dark and almost silent room, the only sounds being beeping machines and old lady snores as I lay alone with my thoughts. I'd had a glimpse of normality spending the afternoon surrounded by some of my best friends but now I felt more alone than ever, just me and the big cancerous tumour residing deep inside of me. I text Karl but he had 'the lads' over to keep him company and watch a boxing match that was on television that night. I was glad he had some company, and relieved that he would get some normality, it was a chance for him to focus on something other than the cancer; but I was jealous and angry that he was living his life without me. I looked on Facebook; picture after picture, status after status of friends and family doing 'normal' things, having fun and living life, whilst my whole world had been put on hold, and in reality I might never get to experience 'normal' life ever again. I was scared, upset and lonely; I cried quietly in that big silent space whilst the rest of the patients slept soundly. I saw on Facebook that Nat was still awake (and a little bit drunk) after staying up to watch the boxing too, so I text her telling her how I was feeling and she immediately tried to ring me. I text back explaining about my bed move so I couldn't talk and she replied with a text saying she was on her way to kidnap me! I think she was serious too. I was giggling as I tried to persuade her it really wasn't a good idea and she continued to insist I was breaking out of there that night whether I liked it or not.

I didn't break out early but I continued to do well with my bag and the incisions were healing well so after eight days the Doctor said I was ready to go home. Karl picked the kids up from school early and brought them to collect me and we were all so excited as the girls helped me pack my belongings and Meadow accidentally stole a hospital bible when I asked her to empty the contents of my bedside table into a bag. Back home I continued with my vegan diet and tried to get used to my colostomy bag whilst we waited for a date to start treatment. Karl surprised me by decorating our bedroom one day whilst I spent the day with my mum getting some new comfy clothes and bits and bobs in preparation for treatment. Mum knew what Karl was up to but managed to keep it a secret from me all day! I loved my new room and it was a good job because I would be spending a lot of time in there once the side effects of the treatment kicked in.

, we got some dates. I was to go to the hospital for a planning day where I would have all sorts of scans and tests done as well as some permanent 'tattoos' on my stomach and hips to ensure that my radiotherapy was done accurately each time. I was also scheduled for a kidney function test the day before to work out just how much of the chemotherapy drugs my body could handle. At the last minute, my appointments were moved to all be on the same morning, to which I asked if this would affect the test results, but was assured it was fine. So, I arranged childcare and I went with Karl and my mum (we were becoming a bit of a team!) to the hospital nice and early. The first thing I had to have done was a blood test and an injection of some sort of radioactive substance that had been specially prepared and came in a little metal container like something from a movie. Then I was to go for my planning scan and tattoos and, in exactly three hours, I would come back for my blood testing again, and that would tell them how well my kidneys were going to tolerate the chemo.

All good Despite me checking twice that all this was OK to happen at the same time, when I arrived at the radiology department, they said that I couldn't have the scan because they also needed to inject some sort of dye into me and it could affect the results of the kidney test. I broke down in tears. In my head this scan was the beginning of my treatment, the beginning of my fight back. The planning appointment was vital to get the ball rolling and prepare my treatment so I could get started, the kidney test could have waited a few more days, but it was too late now I had already had the injection. I was so upset as we waited for my next blood test and I was angry that I had checked twice and had been told it was OK. It turns out for most planning CT scans; contrast dye isn't needed so she wasn't to have known. But I just couldn't cope with yet another delay and I was still upset as I went up for my next blood test. I know it was nothing personal but it just felt like another setback, yet another thing going wrong. Whilst I was in the room with the nurse, who was fighting to get my blood, the phone rang; it was the radiology department asking me to go back down once I was done there. I didn't know what they wanted but I headed straight there and discovered that my mum and Karl had been on a mission, they had talked the staff into doing my planning scan later that afternoon instead of me having to come back the following week. I couldn't thank them enough and we were all relieved as I had my scan and got my new tattoos: four tiny black dots that I will have forever, a permanent reminder of the journey we have been on. It was time for the waiting game again; this time waiting for the green light for treatment to begin.

Whilst I waited I spent a lot of time with my Grandad who was now in a home. This had been a difficult decision to make as a family but Grandad had deteriorated so rapidly since Grandma passed that he needed around the clock care which could be provided by the wonderful home he was now living in. Although never officially diagnosed, Grandad was showing many signs of dementia, at 93 years old he did amazingly well and on good days we caught glimpses of the man he once was, but often he was confused, angry, upset and frightened. Through his confusion he seemed to realise that I was ill again and often asked after me when family went to visit, he was once convinced that I had died and nobody had told him so was very relieved to see me at my next visit. We would sit for hours, he would talk and talk as I listened and tried to make sense of his ramblings, one day he had been busy ruling a country! On other days we would dance, although I was certainly no replacement for his beautiful wife, his dancing queen, but I tried my best with him as my teacher. Spending time with Grandad helped us both, it gave me a kind of escape from everything else that was going on, and it reminded me of how things used to be before all of this heartbreak.

Now we had a bit more of an idea what was going on, it was definitely time to tell the kids exactly what was happening. Of course they knew I had a poorly tummy again and that I'd had a colostomy and now I had to do my business in a little bag attached to my stomach, which they had all had a good look at and tried out for themselves (wearing it, not pooing in one!). But we hadn't actually said the 'c' word again this time round. They were busy dealing with the first ever loss of a loved one and drawing butterflies for Great Grandma in the sky, as well as keeping Great Grandad (and themselves) entertained with regular visits. And of course they had been spending lots of extra time with their Grandma and Grandads, sleepovers and fun days out - they certainly weren't complaining. But we knew by now that my treatment would last at least seven weeks, with hospital every day, some appointments lasting from morning until night. The routine they were all so used to would be changing, with different people picking them up or taking them to school, and later nights or earlier mornings, so that we could make things work.

They needed to know this, and they needed to know that people might ask them questions, look at them with sad faces, or take them out for treats for no particular reason! They needed to know that life was going to change a bit, and that mummy would change a bit too, because mummy had cancer again. We told them I had another bug, another spider in my tummy. Meadow asked straight away "Is it cancer again?" When we answered her honestly she cried "But they said it was gone! How can it come back when they said it was gone?" That was a question I really couldn't answer, and I told her so. Then we told them that this time the doctors were going to use giant laser beams to shoot lasers right through my body and blast that naughty spider away, and once a week I would stay at the hospital all day while they pumped poison into my body to kill him that way too. And then Meadow asked if I was going to die and again I told her "these doctors are amazing, this is their job, they will do all they can to make that spider disappear for good and they have the best machines in the world to help them do that." What more could I say?

That weekend we sat at home watching one of our favourite programmes, snuggled up as a family. Ant and Dec's Saturday Night Takeaway always had us belly laughing and shouting at the TV. Life right now was tough for all of us; full of uncertainties, sadness and pain, but right then, in the moment, we were together as a family, living and loving life and I really couldn't have asked for anything more as I looked around the room at the perfect family we had created. Now wasn't a time to think about how cruel and unfair life could be, I was unbelievably lucky to have been blessed with three perfect children and an amazing husband and there was no way that anyone or anything was going to ruin that for any of us. Then I saw the competition, with a chance to win a holiday to Florida. A family holiday to Disney has always been a dream and now I didn't know if it would ever happen, certainly not any time soon. But then again, it was me that was ill and going through treatment, not the rest of my family, they were just coming along for the ride but didn't they deserve a break? I went on the website and began to fill out the forms, telling our story and nominating my mum and dad to win a 'seat on the plane' with the kids. I didn't tell anybody until it was pretty clear they hadn't won and then I told my mum. I also told her about the competition I had entered on social media to win a 'Mother's Day Afternoon Tea' for mum and me at a local restaurant too - we didn't win that either. "Did you tell them everything?" Mum asked, "About you and your Dad, Grandma dying and Grandad getting ill too?" On both applications I had poured my heart out with all that my poor mum was going through, "That's probably it," she replied, "You should have left some bits out, nobody would believe all of that could happen at once, they probably thought you were lying". Looking back it was a bit crazy, but we got through it and it definitely made us all a hell of a lot stronger.

Chapter 6

I finally began treatment in the middle of March, it felt like we had been waiting such a long time and I was actually quite excited that things were happening at last, but nervous about what the next seven weeks might bring. I had been given my treatment timetable which gave me all the dates and times for my daily radiotherapy and weekly chemotherapy appointments, it even told me which machine I would be using each day and an appointment with my consultant each Monday was scheduled in too. And the best thing, the timetable could be used to get free parking each day in the hospital multi-storey, a massive bonus after the amount we had already spent on hospital parking over the past year and one less thing to worry about. My research told me that the usual course of treatment (if there is such a thing) for cervical cancer patients is external radiotherapy with concurrent Chemotherapy, usually for around five or six weeks, followed by one or two sessions of internal radiotherapy called Brachytherapy. This involves a higher dose of radiotherapy that is given internally to a much more precise area, so as to protect any healthy tissue in the surrounding areas from too much damage. It didn't sound particularly pleasant but it looked like the use of brachytherapy was having a positive impact on cervical cancer outcomes so I accepted it would be part of my journey and I thought about how lucky I am to be living at a time when medicine is so advanced and amazing things are possible. But then I met with my consultant the morning I was due to start my radiotherapy and I mentioned the brachytherapy to her, it turned out I wouldn't be having it after all as my tumour was too big and too widespread so it wasn't suitable for me, I would have two extra weeks of 'normal' external radiotherapy instead. This terrified me; in my head all that she had said right then was "I only give brachytherapy to people who actually have a chance of surviving" and I became fixated on the fact I wasn't going to be having it as if that was going to be the reason my treatment would fail. I googled recent examples of people going through a similar situation and it felt like I was the only woman in the world to not be having brachytherapy as part of my treatment, I couldn't shake off the feeling that this one thing meant I was doomed and there was no hope for me, no matter how many times I was told that this was not the case. I just had to accept that the consultant knew best and get started with my treatment before I drove myself, and my family, any crazier.

Between my mum, Karl and other amazing friends and family members I was chauffeured to the hospital every single day of my treatment, well except for one Saturday towards the end of the seven weeks when Karl was trying to sort out childcare and I snapped and told him I just wanted to go on my own, and so I did. I was just so fed up of being a complete burden to everyone and I felt like my independence was slipping away from me at lightning speed, I couldn't work, I could barely look after my own kids and now I couldn't even be trusted to drive to my own appointments. Yet at the same time I was so thankful for everybody looking after us all so well and making sure I never had to be alone; and I always appreciated the company. I was desperate to be Superwoman, but I guess even superheroes have a sidekick. The first week flew by; I soon got into my radiotherapy routine; a pint of water an hour before my appointment to make sure my bladder was nice and full and everything was in the right place in my pelvis for the lasers to hit all the right spots. When my name was called I would go into a changing room and change into a hospital gown, putting all my belongings into a little basket which I would then take with me when I was called through to my machine. The machine would be all set up ready for me to lay down then any adjustments quickly made using the four tattoos that form a cross on my body. Then everybody would leave the room and watch me through a big window as they first of all scanned my bladder to check it was nicely full, one time a voice through the speaker said "you're bladders like a watermelon I don't know how it hasn't burst!", "I think it might be about to" I replied, right there on the bed, I have never been so desperate in all my life I was in actual pain, "You wouldn't be the first!" I was assured, but thankfully I managed to hold it in for another ten minutes until the machine had finished whirring backwards and forwards around my body as it fired invisible light beams like a weapon of mass destruction. Other days I was sent back to the waiting room to drink more water and wait another hour because my bladder looked more like a deflated balloon, I never seemed to be able to get it just right, and on the days that I did there was usually a delay with the machine meaning I had to go for a wee and start it all again.

That Wednesday I had my first chemo session, and Karl was first on the schedule for 'chemo companion', we'd already been shown the ward and had the whole day explained to us so we knew what to expect. We were also prepared for me to become grumpy, snappy, hungry and irrational, "this will test your marriage" we'd been warned, but Karl said that judging by that list things probably wouldn't be much different. And the sugar-free, vegan diet I had been doing so well at? "You're going to do yourself more damage from the stress of trying to resist a chocolate bar and a big mac, than any harm eating them occasionally whilst you have this treatment could do to your body", my consultant told me. We stopped at McDonalds on the way home that night; a Big Mac has never tasted so good. We had to be at the ward at 8am on chemo day, unless I got a phone call before 7am to say that my bloods weren't good enough for chemo but I never did, and we could expect to be there until around 6pm each time. We'd been told I was welcome to just stay over in the hospital 'hotel' after radiotherapy on a Tuesday night, to save some of the travelling backwards and forwards, but I don't think that option was quite as appealing as it sounds and I wanted to be with my babies although it usually still meant them sleeping out that night to save a super early start in the morning. I just had to keep telling myself that this wasn't forever, in seven short weeks it could even all be over... although I never let myself say that out loud for fear of jinxing it. Chemo day started with me being shown to my comfy reclining chair where I would sit with my arm in a bucket of red hot water, I have my bath and washing up water close to boiling at home so this was not a problem. Once my arm had gone a nice bright pink and the skin looked close to peeling off, a nurse would come along and attempt to insert a big fat needle in to one of my supposedly well prepared veins in order to cannulate my arm ready for treatment. The first week this presented only a very small issue, after a further few minutes in the bucket and a change of nurses, a bit of pain and a few tears I was done and ready to go, as the weeks went on though my poor veins had well and truly had enough and I began to dread this more than anything, although I refused to have a 'port' fitted directly into my chest to make this process easier, preferring to put up with the weekly struggle, the multiple bruises and puncture wounds and the lumpy chemo damaged veins that didn't fully heal for a year.

I looked around the room at other patients, there was such a variety of people, some had come alone and brought a book or an electronic device with headphones, some were sleeping or watching TV and others were sat chatting away with loved ones just like me. They didn't all look like cancer patients, don't get me wrong there were people with no hair or wearing scarves and wigs, but there were also people who looked like they were just having a quick sit down on their way to work, business suits and faces done up, like this was just normal every-day life. I had come in my comfy tracksuit, hair (that thanks to my particular chemo I shouldn't really lose) scraped up in a bun and my face make up free, I probably looked more poorly than any of them and I hadn't even begun yet! The lady in the chair next to me was ready to go as well, with her cannula firmly in place and her lunch menu filled in, she would be there all day like me then I guessed, some of the other people seemed to be leaving already, I had no idea until then that chemo could be a quick half an hour thing! I don't really know what got us chatting but we soon knew all there was to know about each other, Barbara, her brother Dick who had come to stay with her and joined her for all her appointments, Karl and I. Barbara and I were attached to our first huge bottle of fluid, it was literally just fluids, salt solution of some kind that would be pumped into my body over the next couple of hours to help protect my poor kidneys from the lethal poison they, and the whole of my body, were about to be subjected to. We put the world to rights as we all sat there, none of us really knowing what to expect as it was Barbara's first chemo day too, it was also Barbara's first radiotherapy that day so I was able to tell her a little of what to expect although with her cancer being in her lung hers would be quite different we assumed. We spoke about life, about family, about just how shitty and unexpected a cancer diagnosis really is, about the irony of us both sitting there with cancers that are both so heavily related to smokers when neither of us had smoked in our lives.

Barbara would be having her chemo for three days in a row then having a two week break before doing the same again, and she would lose her hair. The wig lady came while we were sat together and we all had a little giggle as she tried some different styles on. Then after lunch it was time for my next bag of fluid, this one helped to line my bladder with a protective film in a bid to minimise the damage, it was thick and black and it hurt, every second of the 30 minutes it took to get into my system it felt like the bones in my arm were being snapped in two, slowing it down relieved the pain slightly but extended the length of time it would take for the bag to empty. The nurses brought around heat blankets but there were never enough to go round although they always made sure I had one just for that half hour of torture then I would quickly pass it on to whoever looked most in need. Next it was anti-sickness tablets and a steroid injection that had a weird reaction of making your bum tingle and gave you a strong taste of metal in your mouth, thankfully only for the 5 minutes it was going in. Then we waited for our own personalised chemo delivery. Barbara's came just before mine, a brown sealed bag that couldn't be exposed to sunlight, her name written on the side as the bag was checked and checked to make sure the right patient was getting the right treatment and no mistakes could possibly be made. I was fascinated to learn that chemo is made up specifically for each individual patient just moments before it is used, mine was the highest strength as my kidneys had shown they could tolerate that, for other patients it would be altered, Barbara was having 'Cisplatin', the same chemo as me, but then she was having another type as well and this was the one that would make her hair fall out. Mine soon arrived and I was hooked up too, I had no idea what to expect, I was anticipating more pain, burning perhaps, I thought it might make me feel instantly ill or that I might have to send Karl to fetch me a sick bowl quick. But it just made me sleepy more than anything, and as I was hooked up to chemo for the next hour I decided I might as well have a little nap whilst Karl went to stretch his legs and get himself some lunch.

After the chemo I then had to have another huge bottle of fluid that over the next couple of hours would flush the chemo straight back out of my system (hoping it had had time to do its cancer-fighting job!) but during this time I was to go down to radiology for today's radiotherapy session, that was always fun with a drip stand trailing behind me as we went down in the lift, I tripped myself and Karl up plenty of times. And then if there was a delay Karl would have to rush back up to get a plug for my drip stand and we would have to budge patients out of the way so I could get near a plug socket. I didn't need to drink water on those days; my poor bladder was full enough with the litres of fluid that had been pumped into it all day and my whole body would be swollen, my eyes looking tiny in my puffed up face. The chemo made my skin yellow; progressively more and more each week until I resembled a chubby yellow hamster, I guessed I probably glowed in the dark too. All patients would be sent home from chemo with their own 'chemo survival kit', mine contained pain relief, anti-sickness and anti-diarrhoea tablets, diuretics and steroids that I took for the next three days and then had a break from for three days until I repeated it all again. And that was chemo day, always the same routine, sometimes with a different companion and usually in a different chair/bed/part of the ward. I took my mum once (well technically she took me, I don't suppose being chosen as chemo companion was a great honour) but she complained about how uncomfortable her chair was when I had a comfy recliner so we did a swap, I didn't take her to chemo day again, not for being a pain in the bum, just because she really does have a bad back and I didn't want her suffering for me. I still dragged her along to many radiotherapy appointments though and pretty much every other appointment too, unless she was needed to look after the kids. The next time, my friend Emma booked the day off work and came, she had packed a bag full of homemade sweet treats, her famous shortbread and juicy strawberries, then in another bag were lots of different craft materials, we made decoupage angels for the kids and some other crafty bits and bobs, that chemo day flew, we even had the nurses joining in. The following week it was Karl again and it was also Barbara's next set of three chemo sessions, we had a wander around the ward and found her and Dick, she had started to lose her hair a bit but she was doing well and we all had a catch up, she had ended up having a port fitted so she didn't have to struggle with cannulas any longer, I had a good look at it but I still wasn't convinced to get one of my own.

At the end of first week I was high on steroids and feeling great, my radiotherapy appointment was late in the day so we took the kids with us after school then we met Sam and Amber for tea, we called it our one week celebration tea and it became a ritual to celebrate each week somehow, a takeaway at home, a meal out or the cinema depending on how I felt, it helped me to remember that it wasn't just about me, the whole family were a part of this but it was so easy to get wrapped up inside my own little routine, floating through it in a bubble and forgetting that life outside still existed. When I saw my consultant exactly one week after treatment had begun I was on cloud nine, I told her how amazing I was feeling, not ill or sick at all, treatment was going well and so far so good. She smiled as she told me this was completely normal, steroids can work wonders and radiotherapy can take a little while to kick in but unfortunately I wasn't to take it as a sign of things to come, most of her patients reacted the same way in the first week. I asked "but what if I really do just get through the whole time feeling well and no issues?" Talk about optimistic. "Sorry Sarah it's not going to happen," she replied, bringing me back down to Earth with a bang. But of course she was right, I slowly but surely began to feel the effects of the treatment. I was losing weight, couldn't tolerate much food and was using regular medication to control sickness and diarrhoea, my first experience of this with a colostomy bag but I will spare you the details. Weekly blood tests became more and more of a struggle, eleven attempts I think being my record to get one measly tube of blood, and it came from the side of my thumb in the end. The radiotherapy machines seemed to be getting more and more temperamental too; the board at reception often displaying delays of ninety minutes or more, turning my ten minutes of radiotherapy in to another long day of waiting around in hospital. Joseph would join us, when he wasn't at nursery, with his packed lunch and bag of toys, he saw it as a fun day out and he got lots of attention from the staff who thought he was super cute. Even now when I say I have a doctor's appointment to go to, he asks if he will need his packed lunch! Joseph met Barbara and Dick one day too when we passed in the radiotherapy corridor, it had become a sort of community, nodding and saying hello to people we saw every day yet barely knew, but we all had so much in common.

On good days it was nice to spend the journey having a catch up with a friend, putting the world to rights in the waiting room and calling for something to eat after, one time Nat came with me and we brought all six kids, we all went to the museum then she stayed there with the kids whilst I nipped over the road for my treatment. But on bad days it was torture not only for me, but I guess for the poor person who I had dragged along with me too, especially my poor friend Anna who, other than my mum and Karl, definitely got me on one of my worst days. From the minute she picked me up I knew I didn't feel right, I thought maybe I was hungry so we sat in the café and had a snack then we went down to radiotherapy and found that my machine was broken so I had been moved to another and there was an indefinite delay. I had already drunk my water but now I needed a wee and nobody could tell me how long it was going to be so I went to the toilet then drunk my water again, then an hour later I had to do the same again, and again an hour after that. We had been there over three hours and I was feeling like death, I could barely talk to Anna but she seemed to understand. I forced her to go for a walk to get herself something to eat whilst I continued to wait, but whilst she was gone, I suddenly got severe stomach cramps and began to cry in agony. The most amazing kind lady who had seen how much I had been struggling for the past couple of hours came and brought me a tissue then gave me a huge hug. Sara was having treatment for cervical cancer too and even to this day we keep in touch, checking up on each other and chatting about things that only people who have been through all we have could possibly understand; I honestly don't know what I would have done without her right at that moment. Anna came rushing back and a nurse took me to another room for a check-up, they thought it might be gall stones and asked me to do a urine sample, they had never seen anything like the sample I gave them. Clear liquid that looked like, in the nurses words "pure water from a mountain spring", if I hadn't of been in so much distress I think they would have thought I was playing a joke on them, filling the bottle with water from the tap. There was no sign of infection and they didn't think it was gall stones after all, "it looks like you've given yourself water poisoning" the Doctor said, I thought she was joking, how could you drink too much water? Apparently you can, and the body doesn't really like it very much if you do, it can in fact be fatal although thankfully not with the amount I had consumed. I finally got to have my radiotherapy after what felt like forever and was very pleased to find my bladder was the perfect size so no more water was required that day. I have barely been able to stomach a glass of plain water since I completed treatment; I always have to have even just a tiny drop of juice in it. Poor Anna was probably traumatised by her experience that day; to be fair it was definitely very different than the picture I had painted for her of a nice afternoon out catching up with her old friend.

As treatment progressed my cancer symptoms were quickly disappearing, the fluid stopped leaking and the low back pains pretty much vanished, the consultant saw these as really encouraging signs but I struggled to share her enthusiasm as for me they were just being replaced with more uncomfortable side effects of treatment and I honestly felt like giving up on days where I could barely make it out my bed to the car. I would sleep all the way to the hospital and Karl would have to help me out the car as my weak body clung to his, my head banging, my mouth and lips sore and a feeling of pins and needles all over my body as the chemo 'worked it's magic' whilst slowly torturing me all at the same time. By week five there were discussions over whether I was well enough for my chemo, my bloods were rubbish, blood counts so low that my body would have struggled to fight off a cold, I was told to ring the hospital immediately if I even started to feel ill in any way, I wasn't even to wait for my temperature to rise. There were many nights when I woke up feeling horrendous and Karl and I had the same debate over and over about whether we needed to find childcare and get to the hospital quickly but it always seemed like too much hassle so we would wait until my radiotherapy appointment the next day and I usually came round a bit by then. Through sheer determination I got through chemo that week, the thought of the strong dose of steroids I would get to take for the next three days definitely helped. Then I saw my Consultant on the Monday and she said enough was enough, putting my poor body through any more chemo would do me more harm than good, maybe I should have been worried about missing two sessions but I was just so relieved it was over. How would I cope without my steroids though? I begged her for more like a heroin addict, she said this sort of addiction was common and prescribed me a course where I would slowly reduce the dose and wean my body off the steroids until I no longer felt like I couldn't live without them.

I continued with my radiotherapy over the next two weeks, it was nice not to have to worry about chemo day and for my health to stabilise a little, maybe even slightly improve. Although I must have been looking particularly crap one day as when I went to let the receptionist know I had arrived for my treatment she told me that she would like to refer me to a free makeup workshop run by a charity called 'Look Good, Feel Good', who aim to support women's self-esteem whilst they are dealing with the effects of cancer treatment on their physical appearance. I decided to take her up on this offer although I was unsure of what to expect and freaking out about the possibility that my 'bag' might play up in the middle of the workshop. But I needn't have worried, I was met by the loveliest group of ladies who immediately welcomed myself and the other patients in and made us feel at home, looking around I felt like a bit of a fraud as I saw ladies with bald heads and headscarves, eyelashes and eyebrows missing. There were other women like me too though, women who might not have lost their hair but were still getting used to looking different in some way; my skin was yellow and my face by now was so bloated and round that I looked like I had been inflated with a pump as if my head was a football. We spent a lovely couple of hours being pampered, relaxing and getting to know one another, it was nice to not have one of my many sidekicks there 'protecting' me, I was fending for myself, talking frankly about the realities of cancer treatment with women who knew just how it felt as right now they were experiencing it too. And it was a bonus at the end of the two hours to walk away with a bag full of goodies, new makeup, perfume and other amazing products; it really did make such a huge difference to my confidence and self-esteem.

With less than two weeks to go the end was in sight and on Bank holiday Monday I had a day off treatment. We decided to have a day out to the seaside and a family day at the races; it was nice just to do something normal, something not related to cancer and treatment. Seeing my babies splashing in the waves as I sat eating chips and taking in the sea air felt like heaven. But I soon started to feel unwell, I put a brave face on for the kids and we really did have the best day but I returned to the car a few times for a quick cat nap and I struggled to ignore the pain beginning to build up in the middle of my back, pressing on my spine like it was being crushed. My head tried desperately to calm me down but the same thought went round and round in my head "the cancer's spreading, it's in your spine, there's nothing anybody can do to save you now".

Chapter 7

As I lay in bed that night there was only one thing on my mind, the pressure in my back was becoming so intense I wasn't able to focus on anything else. I screamed, cried and begged Karl to help me, to take all of our suffering away. He persuaded me to ring the hospital and they told us to go straight over to be seen in the 24 hour oncology ward that was basically an A&E for cancer patients. The lady in the bed next to me was given the news that her cancer had spread to her spine, she must have already been aware her cancer was spreading as both doctor and patient remained very calm, as I tried to hold back the tears at the other side of the curtain. Everybody here seemed so much more poorly than me, I felt like a fraud, like I was wasting everyone's time, I hadn't even finished my treatment yet but I was telling myself to get a grip, to stop making a fuss and just get on with it when there were people so much worse than me right there in that room. When the Doctor came to see me I cried, I was terrified and I poured out everything I had been feeling, emotions I wasn't even aware of flooding out with my tears. "I'm not going to scan you", the Doctor calmly told me, "Your cancer isn't spreading; you have anxiety, because you have been through a hell of a lot!" He tried in vain to tell me it was a horrible but completely normal and expected reaction, I wanted to believe him, to trust him, but I had been told this before by a medical professional...who turned out to be wrong. The Doctor went and got one of the lady consultants who I had met before during my treatment, she sat with me and listened to my whole story again, and then she checked me herself, from head to toe. She agreed that the cancer wasn't spreading, and that the intense pain was a result of a mild backache caused by treatment but made a million times worse by my severe anxiety, but she prescribed me some morphine anyway and told me to go home take some medicine and get a good night sleep before I was back for radiotherapy in the morning. I went home and took the morphine, it got rid of the pain and knocked me straight out but the nightmares it caused were more traumatic than the pain itself and I woke the whole house up screaming and shouting in my sleep, so I didn't bother with the morphine again.

After that things calmed down a bit and I got through the last two weeks of treatment and rang that bell with no real drama! I was still on a low dose of the steroids after becoming slightly addicted and having to be weaned off them but my consultant seemed really pleased with my progress. She assured me that the signs were good and that she had no worries. What I would have given to be in her shoes. I had seen 'the bell' being rung by other patients many times during my treatment, and it always brought a tear to my eye as the whole waiting room erupted into applause. But mine was a bit of an anti-climax; I was the last appointment of the day so it was a good job I had brought my family with me because my only other witnesses were a receptionist and a cleaner! We didn't break our tradition, all heading for a family meal as our final weekly celebration. I suddenly felt more tired than ever, it was surreal; I had been in my treatment bubble for so long I hadn't really given a thought to what would happen after. It's a strange feeling finishing treatment, it doesn't automatically mean you are better, yet everybody else seems to think of it that way. Text after text of congratulations and celebration but all I could think was "what is there to celebrate? What if it hasn't worked, or it comes back, what could possibly happen next?" It would be a long 12 weeks before I had the answers I so desperately craved because treatment carries on working for at least 3 months after you have finished, so to scan too early would mean a chance of seeing something that was yet to disappear.

I managed a full 24 hours away from the hospital before I began having issues that meant an overnight admission and a CT scan of my bowel. "We don't really know what it is, but it could be a tumour in your bowel, although it could be as a result of treatment; let's just wait and see," the Doctor told us, whilst the same old fear crept over my skin giving me a feeling that the spider from within was crawling all over me, invading every part of my body and causing irreversible damage and destruction. Karl had to go home to look after my poor babies who had only had their mummy to themselves for one short day; I lay awake all night, desperately but unsuccessfully trying to focus on something other than the constant voice repeating over and over that the cancer was spreading fast. The next day it was my own consultant who entered the room with a grin on her face, I was exhausted and confused, what could she possibly have to smile about?? "You can go home!" she said, "It's too early for me to tell you this officially Sarah but there is NO EVIDENCE OF TUMOUR on the CT scan that was performed last night, you have a hole in your bowel as we expected may happen so we will keep an eye on that but you can go home and enjoy some much needed time with your family". You can't imagine how happy I was to be diagnosed with a hole in my bowel!

The next side-effect I waited not so enthusiastically for was the menopause. I was lucky during my hysterectomy to have kept my ovaries, and so far they had continued to work just fine, but after seven weeks of intensive radiotherapy they had now been well and truly damaged beyond repair and I was warned to look out for signs of an inevitable premature menopause. At just 31 years of age. It started with the hot flushes, less than a month after completing treatment, to begin with I thought maybe it was just due to the weather warming up but, unless I was now living in the Sahara Desert, it soon became clear it was more than just a heatwave. I remember my mum once describing a hot flush as waking up in the night with the urge just to strip off completely and run outside naked (an urge I hope she never acted upon), and that's exactly how it felt! I would be snug in bed, fast asleep, then 'boom', wide awake and on fire! Karl could feel the heat radiating from me as he got out of bed for the tenth time that night to switch on my fan for me. I probably had other signs too but they would have been so similar to the nausea, memory loss, brain fog and grumpiness that I was already experiencing thanks to the chemo, that it all just rolled into one. I didn't have to put up with this for long though as I was given no choice but to begin using hormone replacement therapy (HRT). Going into the menopause around twenty years before my body would be naturally ready poses its own issues, the decrease in estrogen levels can lead to heart disease and a significantly higher risk of osteoporosis, meaning my bones need protection to help reduce the chances of them cracking and crumbling as I reach old age. My poor pelvis has already been through so much with the amount of radiotherapy that has been fired through it and there's already a risk that I could suffer from radiation induced cracks in the pelvic bone that may even appear years down the line, so it was important that I started on treatment as soon as possible to help protect my bones best we could. I get my estrogen from HRT patches, clear squares that I stick on my body and change twice a week in a bid to counteract the effects of the menopause. I can only stick them below my waist though, never near my chest, as the use of HRT brings with it a risk of other illnesses, especially when used for an extended period of time, one of these being breast cancer, alongside an increased risk of blood clots and strokes. As well as the many other side-effects I could expect to experience as a result of my chemo and radiotherapy, they also come with a risk of more cancer.....just another type. It's no wonder my anxiety was on overdrive.

I don't like using synthetic hormones, just as I don't like having a colostomy bag, both my patch and my bag are a daily reminder of all that I've been through. But they are also a reminder of all that I have overcome. I would rather be here to wear the patch and change the bag than the alternative. It upsets me to have been left infertile, although of course I appreciate just how lucky I am to have my three beautiful children every single day, and I really don't think I would have ever chosen to have anymore. But to have that choice taken away from me is still difficult to accept. My mind plays tricks on me, telling me that I would have had another baby if I could, and I lay awake at night wondering how I would feel if Karl and I were to break up and he went on to have more children with somebody less broken than me. Of course cancer, the menopause and everything else that has come with it, especially my anxiety, has had a huge impact on our intimate relationship. I'm sure for a long time Karl felt more like my carer than my husband, not what you expect less than five years into married life. At times I pushed him away, physically disgusted at the thought and sight of my own body, other times I just had no desire whatsoever, especially when my head was so full of worry and fear. I convinced myself that being intimate with my own husband would cause my cancer to come back and nothing I read, or was told by my consultant, could convince me otherwise. I was terrified of being in pain, of bleeding, but most of all of somehow causing the cancer to return. It's taken a long time, a lot of stress and frustration, to deal with these issues. I'm just so grateful for the love and patience of my amazing husband, who remains by my side no matter what.

With summer approaching it was the perfect time to rest and recuperate with my beautiful family and thanks to my friend Danielle, we went to a caravan for a few days just to get away from everything and be together, I was still exhausted and did plenty of sleeping but it was so nice to have a change of scenery and to spend some time focussing solely on the kids, Joseph turned 4 whilst we were away and, of course, was spoilt rotten. And then, we got back to the news that some of our amazing friends had been fundraising through online raffles whilst I was undergoing treatment and had raised enough money to send us abroad! We were gobsmacked, neither Karl or I felt very comfortable with the idea at first as we really didn't want the attention or for people to go out of their ways for us, but our babies absolutely deserved it and our friends weren't taking no for an answer. They talked about booking for us to go to Disneyland Paris, but I had to be realistic and explain that there was no way I would manage it, so we opted for a week long holiday to Spain instead, where I would be able to relax as we created some amazing family memories.

Whilst we waited for my MRI scan and official treatment results, we held a fun day in the local community to raise money for some of the charities and teams that had treated me, it was all the idea of one of my best friends Michelle, the same friend who had been a huge part of raising the money for our holiday, but in the end so many of our friends and family got involved, running games and stalls, serving food and drinks, donating prizes and we even arranged a charity football match that was such a success players were having to swap about to ensure everyone could take part. So many people attended, there was a huge buzz around the event; it was a red hot day and the most perfect celebration, where not only our friends and family but the whole community came together as one. We spent the day surrounded by happiness, positivity and love and through the event we raised over £800 thanks to the generosity of our own community. I sent a large amount of the money as a donation to the hospital I was treated at and asked that some of it be used to buy more heat blankets for the chemo ward to help keep treatment as comfortable as possible for future patients, this was the first thing that came to my mind when I was thinking about how my treatment could have been made even a little bit easier. Before cancer I was always getting itchy feet, talking about moving away, looking online at where we could live that would be better than the town we live in. I never wanted to be at home on a weekend, always searching for things to do and places to go. I remember at the end of that special day, when I was on an absolute high, I thought "where in this world could I ever live in a community as amazing as this one?" We have recently bought a new house... in the community we know and love.

That summer flew and it was soon time for the all-important MRI and Pet CT scans, the only difficult decision I had to make now was whether to get my results before or after our holiday! I finally settled on 17th August, just a couple of days before we went away and also the exact same date that I had received my first 'all clear' a year previously. At the time I saw this as a good sign, a sign that this date would become a special date for us in the future, a date to be celebrated as an anniversary of the day I got the all clear....twice. And to start with, it was. All my scans were clear, the signs were all positive that the spider had been eradicated once more and I finally managed to relax a little as I packed for our well needed week in the sun. I did my best to relax in Spain, I struggled to eat much, was easily exhausted, couldn't drink alcohol and suffered with awful stomach cramps as a result of my treatment and I was still very much getting used to life with a colostomy bag so going abroad with one was a whole new experience. But despite all that we had an amazing holiday and made so many memories, the kids loved every second and it was so nice to give them the focus they deserved. It was the first time we had been abroad as a family and the first time Joseph had been on an aeroplane so he was just in awe of the whole experience. But then we got back and my anxiety got the better of me, I became fixated on the fact that I had received the results on the same date and I was absolutely convinced that this meant history was going to repeat itself again on the date I was told of my recurrence in February. Returning to work in September 2017 gave me a bit of a distraction but whenever I wasn't there my thoughts would return to these dates and I was obsessed with finding things wrong with my health. Over the next couple of months I had chest x-rays, saw a breast specialist and had countless trips to visit my GP over lumps, bumps, coughs, aches and pains that I convinced myself each time were another recurrence of cancer.

It was another difficult Christmas as I dragged myself around the shops, trying so hard to get excited and 'into the Christmas spirit'. But it just wasn't happening. As well as being convinced I was ill again, I was also sure that this was the last Christmas I would ever have. I cried as I wrapped gifts for my loved ones, then I forced a smile whenever my babies were around. Christmas day was hard, I made sure the kids had no idea how I was feeling and of course it was a really special day for them, but by the end of the day I was exhausted and emotional as I headed to bed for an early night. Life felt harder than ever and the guilt I felt every single day was like torture. I wanted to just go back to life before cancer, either that or just not be here at all, because at that time I couldn't see any sort of future for me, and I was angry that (in my head) my children were facing a future without me in it. Nobody understood. My friends thought I should be happy, grateful and living life to the max. If only it was that simple! I worried about everything, about my friends, my family, I completely over reacted every time my children even sneezed; it felt like I was on the edge waiting for the next thing to spiral out of my control.

away; it takes time and a hell of a lot of effort to learn to live with it remaining a massive part of your life.

My GP put me on the waiting list for some counselling, I had tried counselling before, when I was going through treatment, at a local cancer support centre, but for whatever reason I didn't really feel that particular counselling was right for me I did however love having reflexology sessions which is something the centre also offer as part of a selection of therapies with volunteer therapists. I tried to keep myself busy with the kids and work and pushed those thoughts to the back of my mind. And in March 2018 I went back to work in a school with the intention of progressing on to completing my NQT year as soon as the opportunity arose. I had finally begun to calm down a little when history hadn't repeated itself after all and I was now well past the date in February that I had been diagnosed the second time the previous year; a date that had caused me so much anxiety and so many sleepless nights. It actually felt like some sort of new normality had begun to resume. Working at the same school my children attended allowed for a good work/life balance and things were feeling pretty positive, I was even beginning to allow myself to think about a future that I now finally believed I might one day get to live.

Then in April we lost Grandad and it felt like the end of an era. Of course we were sad but also relieved that he was no longer suffering and we all like to think he is back with my Grandma where he belongs. I miss them both so much and think about them every day, with all that was going on it was as if they both just slipped away in the middle of the chaos. Mum struggled to know what to do with herself after devoting her life to caring for us all for so long. I was a year in remission, back at work and trying my best to get on with life, dad was doing well and enjoying retirement and mum was suddenly a bit lost, she was also semi-retired so had lots of time to do anything she liked, but after so long spent attending hospital appointments, being a taxi service, helping with the kids, visiting and non-stop worrying she wasn't really sure what it was she liked or wanted to do anymore. She settled for doing my ironing and cleaning, I didn't complain. My 12 month MRI came in May and the results again gave us and the consultant further reassurance, and hope. Life felt like it was finally on the up and I was enjoying working in the school nursery with a really lovely team of staff who encouraged me to apply for a full time teaching position in the reception class to begin that September, I really felt that now was the right time and a couple of weeks later I found out the job was mine!

Chapter 8

I spent the summer of 2018 preparing for my first experience of life as a 'proper' teacher, although the highlight of the summer was most definitely our holiday to Turkey to be at our best friend's sides as Natalie and Karl took their wedding vows. So many amazing memories were made with the most fantastic friends and family, without a doubt an experience we will never ever forget. But whilst we were away I could feel my anxiety starting to creep back, I tried my hardest to keep it at bay whilst we were in Turkey and when we got home I threw myself into my new venture, preparing my classroom and getting myself as teacher ready as possible! My colostomy bag was a worry, what if it played up during the day when I was on my own with a class of thirty children? What if it made a noise and the children heard it? Or even worse the other staff, or parents?? The weekly staff meeting set my anxiety off so much I would nearly cry at the thought of having to go to it just in-case my bag misbehaved. I very quickly became exhausted from my increasing anxiety and the sheer number of hours I was working, both in work and at home, and my family were starting to suffer. Meadow was now also displaying signs of anxiety and it had come to her with a vengeance, to the point that her suffering even reduced me to tears at work on more than one occasion, and Joseph was desperate for his mummy back and misbehaving at home and at school. And to top it all off I just wasn't getting the support I needed as an NQT, I wasn't able to be the teacher I knew I could be as there were so many differences of opinion and ways of working, it just wasn't working out and I found myself clamming up at work, not really knowing what to do or say, struggling to have a conversation never-mind teach a class of children to the best of my ability. I began to dread getting up and going to work each morning, I was miserable, I was lost, and all I knew was that I had not fought so hard to be here to feel like this. I had been discussing all of this with the counsellor I had finally started seeing after over six months on the waiting list, and she was concerned about my lack of self-confidence and my constant need for reassurance, she thought that I was too hard on myself and that I had taken on way too much too soon. I just felt like a complete failure, in every aspect of life. And the guilt I again felt about anything and everything was slowly consuming me.

A couple of days before the first half-term holiday I was doing some small group reading with some children when a senior member of staff came and sat close and began to observe me, I couldn't cope, I had no idea that this was about to happen and I could feel a panic attack rising up through my body, my skin tingling and my head close to exploding. I tried desperately to carry on reading with the children but all I really wanted to do was scream and run. This wasn't fair on me or the children, it wasn't fair on my own family either I needed to spend my week off making some serious decisions about all of the important things in my life and if that meant giving up my job, then so be it, my own and my families health and happiness was and always will be top of my list. The next day I felt ill, every part of me hurt, I had a temperature and all the scary thoughts came spiralling back through my mind. I knew I was poorly again, in some way or another.

We spent our week off on a Mediterranean cruise with my parents and Sam and Amber, it was the last cruise ship my grandparents had holidayed on and we took their ashes to scatter them together at sea. I was on antibiotics for a sinus infection but still managed to have the most wonderful, relaxing time. One afternoon, Meadow, Phoebe and Joseph, all went to the on board kids club and the six of us adults headed to the spa for a couple of hours of tranquillity and relaxation. We sat in the hot tub chatting when, I can't remember who suggested it, but we decided to call it the 'honesty pool'. We took turns going round the pool and 'confessing' anything we wanted to each other. It was my turn. "I don't want to be a teacher", I said, "I'm not happy, I hate my job and I never wanted to be a teacher anyway, I wanted to be a midwife, that's my biggest regret". I didn't know what sort of response to expect, but the one I got absolutely blew me away. "Quit, if you're not happy Sarah, quit". "Why haven't you told us, you haven't mentioned it for so many years!" "As soon as we get back from this holiday let's find out how we can make that dream come true".

I handed in my notice the first week back, with my amazing, supportive family on board there was no going back. Then I had some worrying bleeding (which I completely overreacted to of course) which resulted in me having to have a minor procedure where it was discovered I have radiation proctitis to my bowel, irritation caused by the radiation I received during treatment. It really isn't anything to worry about but it does mean that any chance of ever having my colostomy reversed was now gone. I had a few days off work after my procedure but I knew there was no way I was ready to go back. Meadow was still struggling with her emotions and anxiety to the point she burst into tears every time she saw me and unless she was at school she couldn't bear to leave my side. Life truly was exhausting and enough was enough, I booked an appointment with my GP and poured my heart out to him, once I started I just couldn't stop, the tears were flowing as I tried to somehow explain that my biggest fear was that I would die but my greatest desire was to be dead. I felt responsible for the stress and anxiety that so many members of my family were experiencing and I was physically and mentally exhausted, I just wanted to take everybody's stress and pain away and set them free so they could live a normal life again. I told him I knew my cancer was going to come back and kill me anyway so it just didn't make sense to prolong the torture and pain for everyone. I told him I thought I was crazy but he told me I most definitely wasn't.

The Doctor diagnosed a form of post-traumatic stress as a result of all I have been through, he suggested medication but I was really reluctant and told him I would think about it, and discuss it with Karl. He gave me a sick note for a month but warned me that he wouldn't be saying I was fit for work until he truly believed I was ready, whether that be six weeks or six months. I was relieved in a way that I would never be teaching again, but I was stuck so far inside my own thoughts and worries that it was more just a relief that a small amount of space had been freed inside my mind... which of course I quickly filled with more worry. This time it was an ache in my leg that I just couldn't stop thinking about, it started off as a small ache in my thigh but it soon consumed my every thought. At first I thought the aching thigh was swelling and was now bigger than my other thigh, a sign of lymphedema, a common condition caused by the treatment I had undergone. So I bought a tape measure and obsessively measured it, but when it turned out both thighs remained the same size my anxious mind decided I had bone cancer, I knew it, but nobody would listen or believe me. I drove my mum crazy with my constant obsession with this ache in my leg, on my birthday she said enough was enough and she took me to see a doctor. Again I cried as I told the doctor that I didn't mean to upset anyone or go on and on about it but I was convinced that I needed a bone scan because my cancer had spread. She told me it was time for medication, not just for my sake but for the sake of my whole family, I had no choice but to agree. Even now when my anxiety rears its ugly head I see the stress it causes Karl and the guilt instantly returns. I know none of this is my fault, but that doesn't matter, it's because of me that so many lives have been affected and I still find this difficult to accept and live with.

After all my reservations the medication worked wonders, that and some time off work to destress, I was getting my life back again, even my counsellor couldn't believe the huge leaps of progress I was making. After an unexpected week in a hotel, where we celebrated three of our birthdays! We moved into our new home and had the most relaxing family Christmas. Then in January this year (2019) I went back to work three days a week at the nursery I had previously worked at with Nat as my manager. Meadows anxiety, although it has its blips, has improved massively and she no longer has to see the counsellor she had been seeing at school. We no longer have concerns over Joseph's behaviour either, not that he's perfect but he's back to being a typical six year old boy! And we are back to being a happy and content family (most of the time!) I'm still working part time in the nursery but thanks to the absolutely unforgettable support of my family I begin training to be a midwife this September! A dream I have always had and for lots of reasons never believed would ever come true, it really is never too late. Dad is doing amazingly well, he has just been signed off by his oncologist and is back to having blood tests through his GP and Mum is doing good she's slowly learning to relax and take life a little bit easier, we are all looking forward to Sam and Amber's wedding in August! I have also just had my second year all clear, meaning my check-ups now go from three monthly to four, more often than would usually be the case but I'm still classed as high risk for recurrence and because of how rare my circumstances were nobody can really say what will happen next. If my cancer was to return then I would have a different treatment plan, I could never have radiotherapy in the same place again, of course that scares me but for now I'm doing well, I have no signs of recurrence and I've done pretty well so far by not suffering with too many side effects as a result of my treatment, so it's all a step in the right direction and we couldn't be happier right now. I don't know what the future holds for me or for anybody but I certainly no longer take it for granted that I will get one, we have been shown that life is for living and this family plan to do just that.

I've found that since having cancer I've become a little bit more 'selfish', or maybe that's the wrong word, I now put myself and my loved ones first and I've learnt to say no! I no longer go out of my way to make people happy when I know they wouldn't do the same for me, I focus more on the happiness of my close friends and family, and myself. I give myself time on my own, time to relax and re-energise; I did try yoga for a short time as it was recommended by my consultant to help my body recover but I would spend the whole session worrying about my bag embarrassing me by making a loud noise, so I really didn't get much benefit from it. I prefer to go to the gym or exercise on my own at home, doing a bit of Zumba with my girls. I enjoy more quality time with my friends now, making plans and saying 'yes' to social events that before would have taken me too far out of my comfort zone. I don't let the little things get to me as much but at the same time I have much less tolerance for bullshit! I won't waste my time listening to lies and negative opinions, gossip or rumours. Having cancer has shown me what really matters and just how precious life is and I am absolutely determined not to waste a minute of it. It's not always easy but the good times now feel better than ever before, and it really is getting easier with time. I have learnt to accept there will be blips along the way but I now feel confident we will get through them together.

Meadow still has her struggles but I'm in a much better place to help and support her with them, she makes us proud every day with her enthusiasm for learning and making a difference in the world, from the 'Race for Life' she arranged at school to her mission to recycle and use less plastic to help save the planet. My little fairy princess Phoebe just gets on with life, she amazes us with her huge heart full of love and kindness, she's just the most caring and loyal friend anybody could wish for. I worry sometimes about her keeping things bottled up inside, and that one day she might just explode, but if she did then I know this family would take it all in our stride, pull together and support her through it just as we have each other. Then there's my boy Joseph, my baby (sorry Mum!), he was so young when I first got the spider in my tummy and I'm sure he doesn't really remember much about it! But he's the one who makes us all smile when life gets tough, with his silly dances, his funny comments and his enthusiasm for life, he keeps us all going and melts our hearts with just one look. And Karl, my husband, my best friend and soulmate, I could write pages and pages but I will just say thank you. For everything. I'm eternally grateful for all that these precious people bring into my world, I will forever be in their debt and couldn't begin to imagine where I would be right now without them. I look forward to the most amazing future with all of my friends and family by my side.

So, this is me. I have a little bag attached to my stomach which sometimes makes noises that I can't control, usually at the quietest most inappropriate moments, or fills up like a balloon, bulging out under my clothes. I'm living without pretty much every body part that makes me female, even my right boob is fake but that's another story. But I'm also a mum, a wife, a daughter, a sister, a friend, thanks to the amazing doctors and nurses who fixed me. I'm a little bit older, an awful lot wiser and in the end, I'm happier. After everything my family has been through, we appreciate every little thing and we understand just how important it is to spend our time here loving and living life to its fullest. Thank you, cancer, for making me a better person, but I would really appreciate it if we never have to see you again.

Sarah

x

The Spider in Mummy's Tummy.
(Through the eyes of 3 year old Joseph)

There's a spider in mummy's tummy,
How did it get there?
Nobody knows.
I think when she was sleeping,
It crawled right up her nose

Mummy said the doctors
Will try to get it out,
With laser beams and big machines,
He best not hang about!

Mum goes to the hospital
Sometimes I go too,
With books and toys and jigsaws
There's lots to see and do.

Then I open up my lunch box
And I sit down right beside her,
I share my lunch with mummy
But never with her spider!

I wonder what he does in there,
Does he do jigsaws too?
Or maybe he is sleeping,
I hope he doesn't poo!

It makes me feel quite sad sometimes,
Spiders can be scary!
I wonder if it's small and cute,
Or big and fat and hairy.

Sometimes mummy's tired
And she has to take a rest,
But that's ok coz mummy cuddles
Really are the best.

You have a sleep mummy
I will watch TV,
I just love being with you,
And all our family.

Mummy you look different,
Some things are not the same.
But I've checked and it's still you mum,
You know our favourite games.

I'm getting mad and angry now,
This spider is so bad.
He's making my mum poorly
And all my family sad.

Those doctor's best just shoot him quick
With their laser beams,
Or make him drink their poison
Till we hear his spider screams!

But I know it isn't his fault,
Nobody's to blame,
I just want my mummy back
To play our favourite games.

The Doctor's said they've done it!
The Spiders disappeared!
I hope he doesn't come again
Coz... He was a little weird.

Mummy's feeling better now,
And so are we.
Now you're feeling better mum,
What's for tea?

Printed in Great Britain
by Amazon